Contents

Tortilla Crunch Chicken Fingers

1 envelope LIPTON® RECIPE SECRETS® Savory Herb with Garlic Soup Mix
1 cup finely crushed plain tortilla chips or cornflakes (about 3 ounces)
1½ pounds boneless, skinless chicken breasts, cut into strips
1 egg
2 tablespoons water
2 tablespoons I CAN'T BELIEVE IT'S NOT BUTTER!® Spread, melted

1. Preheat oven to 400°F.

2. In medium bowl, combine soup mix and tortilla chips. In large plastic bag or bowl, combine chicken and egg beaten with water until evenly coated. Remove chicken and dip in tortilla mixture until evenly coated; discard bag. On 15½×10½×1-inch jelly-roll pan sprayed with nonstick cooking spray, arrange chicken; drizzle with I Can't Believe It's Not Butter!® Spread. Bake uncovered 12 minutes or until chicken is thoroughly cooked. Serve with chunky salsa, if desired.

Makes about 24 chicken fingers

Party Stuffed Pinwheels

**1 envelope LIPTON® RECIPE SECRETS® Savory Herb with Garlic Soup
  Mix***

1 package (8 ounces) cream cheese, softened

1 cup shredded mozzarella cheese (about 4 ounces)

2 tablespoons milk

1 tablespoon grated Parmesan cheese

2 packages (10 ounces each) refrigerated pizza crust

*Also terrific with LIPTON® RECIPE SECRETS® Onion Soup Mix.

1. Preheat oven to 425°F. In medium bowl, combine all ingredients
except pizza crusts; set aside.

2. Unroll pizza crusts, then top evenly with filling. Roll, starting at
longest side, jelly-roll style. Cut into 32 rounds.**

3. On baking sheet sprayed with nonstick cooking spray, arrange
rounds cut side down.

4. Bake uncovered 13 minutes or until golden brown.

Makes 32 pinwheels

**If rolled pizza crusts are too soft to cut, refrigerate or freeze until firm.

Sweet Pepper Pizza Fingers

2 tablespoons margarine or butter
2 large red, green and/or yellow bell peppers, thinly sliced
1 clove garlic, finely chopped
1 envelope LIPTON® RECIPE SECRETS® Onion Soup Mix
1 cup water
1 package (10 ounces) refrigerated pizza crust
1½ cups shredded mozzarella cheese (about 6 ounces), divided

1. Preheat oven to 425°F.

2. In 12-inch skillet, melt margarine over medium heat; cook peppers and garlic, stirring occasionally, 5 minutes or until peppers are tender. Stir in soup mix blended with water. Bring to a boil over high heat. Reduce heat to low and simmer uncovered 6 minutes or until liquid is absorbed. Remove from heat; set aside to cool 5 minutes.

3. Meanwhile, on baking sheet sprayed with nonstick cooking spray, roll out pizza crust into 12×8-inch rectangle. Sprinkle 1 cup mozzarella cheese over crust; top with cooked pepper mixture, spreading to edges of dough. Top with remaining ½ cup mozzarella cheese. Bake 10 minutes or until crust is golden brown and topping is bubbly. Remove from oven and let stand 5 minutes. To serve, cut into 4×1-inch strips. *Makes about 24 fingers*

Hearty Nachos

1 pound ground beef
1 envelope LIPTON® RECIPE SECRETS® Onion Soup Mix
1 can (19 ounces) black beans, rinsed and drained
1 cup prepared salsa
1 package (8½ ounces) plain tortilla chips
1 cup shredded Cheddar cheese (about 4 ounces)

1. In 12-inch nonstick skillet, brown ground beef over medium-high heat; drain.

2. Stir in soup mix, black beans and salsa. Bring to a boil over high heat. Reduce heat to low and simmer 5 minutes or until heated through.

3. Arrange tortilla chips on serving platter. Spread beef mixture over chips; sprinkle with Cheddar cheese. Top, if desired, with sliced green onions, sliced pitted ripe olives, chopped tomato and chopped cilantro.   *Makes 8 servings*

**SIMPLE
STARTERS**

Can't Get Enough Chicken Wings

18 chicken wings (about 3 pounds)
1 envelope LIPTON® RECIPE SECRETS® Savory Herb with Garlic Soup Mix
½ cup water
2 to 3 tablespoons hot pepper sauce* (optional)
2 tablespoons butter or margarine

Use more or less hot pepper sauce as desired.

1. Cut tips off chicken wings. (Save tips for soup, if desired.) Cut chicken wings in half at joint. Deep fry, bake or broil until golden brown and crunchy.

2. Meanwhile, in small saucepan, combine soup mix, water and hot pepper sauce. Cook over low heat, stirring occasionally, 2 minutes or until thickened. Remove from heat and stir in butter.

3. In large bowl, toss cooked chicken wings with hot soup mixture until evenly coated. Serve, if desired, over greens with cut-up celery.

Makes 36 appetizers

7-Layer Ranch Dip

1 envelope LIPTON® RECIPE SECRETS® Ranch Soup Mix
1 container (16 ounces) sour cream
1 cup shredded lettuce
1 medium tomato, chopped (about 1 cup)
1 can (2.25 ounces) sliced pitted ripe olives, drained
¼ cup chopped red onion
1 can (4.5 ounces) chopped green chilies, drained
1 cup shredded Cheddar cheese (about 4 ounces)

1. In 2-quart shallow dish, combine soup mix and sour cream.

2. Evenly layer remaining ingredients, ending with cheese. Chill, if desired. Serve with tortilla chips. *Makes 7 cups dip*

Creamy Garlic Salsa Dip

1 envelope LIPTON® RECIPE SECRETS® Savory Herb with Garlic Soup Mix*
1 container (16 ounces) sour cream
½ cup your favorite prepared salsa

*Also terrific with LIPTON® RECIPE SECRETS® Onion Soup Mix.

1. In medium bowl, combine all ingredients; chill if desired.

2. Serve with your favorite dippers.

Makes 2½ cups dip

DYNAMITE DIPS

Three Bean Salsa

1 envelope LIPTON® RECIPE SECRETS® Savory Herb with Garlic Soup
  Mix
½ cup water
1 large tomato, chopped
1 cup drained canned red kidney or cannellini beans
1 cup drained canned black or pinto beans
1 cup drained canned garbanzo beans or chick-peas
2 teaspoons white or white wine vinegar (optional)

In 12-inch skillet, blend soup mix with water. Bring to a boil over high
heat; stir in tomato. Reduce heat to low and simmer 3 minutes. Stir in
beans and simmer 3 minutes or until heated through. Stir in vinegar.
Garnish, if desired, with chopped fresh parsley or cilantro.

Makes about 4 cups salsa

Serving Suggestion: *Serve as a side dish or as a topping with
grilled poultry, beef, lamb or pork.*

DYNAMITE DIPS

Hot Artichoke Dip

1 envelope LIPTON® RECIPE SECRETS® Onion Soup Mix*
1 can (14 ounces) artichoke hearts, drained and chopped
1 cup HELLMANN'S® or BEST FOODS® Mayonnaise
1 container (8 ounces) sour cream
1 cup shredded Swiss or mozzarella cheese (about 4 ounces)

**Also terrific with LIPTON® RECIPE SECRETS® Savory Herb with Garlic, Golden*
Onion, or Onion Mushroom Soup Mix.

1. Preheat oven to 350°F. In 1-quart casserole, combine all
ingredients.

2. Bake uncovered 30 minutes or until heated through.

3. Serve with your favorite dippers.   *Makes 3 cups dip*

Cold Artichoke Dip: *Omit Swiss cheese. Stir in, if desired, ¼ cup*
grated Parmesan cheese. Do not bake.

Recipe Tip: *When serving hot dip for a party, try baking it in*
2 smaller casseroles. When the first casserole is empty, replace it
with the second one, fresh from the oven.

White Pizza Dip

1 envelope LIPTON® RECIPE SECRETS® Savory Herb with Garlic Soup Mix
1 container (16 ounces) sour cream
1 cup (8 ounces) ricotta cheese
1 cup shredded mozzarella cheese (about 4 ounces), divided
¼ cup (1 ounce) chopped pepperoni
1 loaf Italian or French bread, sliced

1. Preheat oven to 350°F. In shallow 1-quart casserole, combine soup mix, sour cream, ricotta cheese, ¾ cup mozzarella cheese and pepperoni.

2. Sprinkle with remaining ¼ cup mozzarella cheese.

3. Bake uncovered 30 minutes or until heated through. Serve with bread.   *Makes 3 cups dip*

DYNAMITE DIPS

13

Perfect Party Spinach Dip

1 envelope LIPTON® RECIPE SECRETS® Vegetable Soup Mix*
1 container (8 ounces) regular or light sour cream
1 cup HELLMANN'S® or BEST FOODS® Real Mayonnaise
1 package (10 ounces) frozen chopped spinach, thawed and
  squeezed dry
1 can (8 ounces) water chestnuts, drained and chopped (optional)

Also terrific with LIPTON® RECIPE SECRETS® Savory Herb with Garlic Soup Mix.

1. In medium bowl, combine all ingredients; chill at least 2 hours.

2. Serve with your favorite dippers.   *Makes 3 cups dip*

DYNAMITE DIPS

Hot French Onion Dip

1 envelope LIPTON® RECIPE SECRETS® Onion Soup Mix
1 container (16 ounces) sour cream
2 cups shredded Swiss cheese (about 8 ounces), divided
¼ cup HELLMANN'S® or BEST FOODS® Mayonnaise

1. Preheat oven to 375°F. In 1-quart casserole, combine soup mix, sour cream, 1¾ cups Swiss cheese and mayonnaise.

2. Bake uncovered 20 minutes or until heated through. Sprinkle with remaining ¼ cup cheese.

3. Serve, if desired, with sliced French bread or your favorite dippers.

Makes 2 cups dip

DYNAMITE DIPS

15

Garlic 'n Lemon Roast Chicken

1 small onion, finely chopped
1 envelope LIPTON® RECIPE SECRETS® Savory Herb with Garlic Soup Mix
2 tablespoons BERTOLLI® Olive Oil
2 tablespoons lemon juice
1 (3½-pound) roasting chicken

1. In large plastic bag or bowl, combine onion and soup mix blended with oil and lemon juice; add chicken. Close bag and shake, or toss in bowl, until chicken is evenly coated. Cover and marinate in refrigerator, turning occasionally, 2 hours.

2. Preheat oven to 350°F. Place chicken and marinade in 13×9-inch baking or roasting pan. Arrange chicken, breast side up; discard bag.

3. Bake uncovered, basting occasionally, 1 hour and 20 minutes or until meat thermometer reaches 180°F. (Insert meat thermometer into thickest part of thigh between breast and thigh; make sure tip does not touch bone.)   *Makes 4 servings*

Crab-Stuffed Chicken Breasts

1 package (8 ounces) cream cheese, softened
6 ounces frozen crabmeat or imitation crabmeat, thawed and
   drained
1 envelope LIPTON® RECIPE SECRETS® Savory Herb with Garlic Soup
   Mix
6 boneless, skinless chicken breast halves (about 1½ pounds)
¼ cup all-purpose flour
2 eggs, beaten
¾ cup plain dry bread crumbs
2 tablespoons BERTOLLI® Olive Oil
1 tablespoon I CAN'T BELIEVE IT'S NOT BUTTER!® Spread

1. Preheat oven to 350°F. Combine cream cheese, crabmeat and soup mix; set aside. With knife parallel to cutting board, slice horizontally through each chicken breast, stopping 1 inch from opposite edge; open breasts. Evenly spread each breast with cream cheese mixture. Close each chicken breast, securing open edge with wooden toothpicks.

2. Dip chicken in flour, then eggs, then bread crumbs, coating well. In 12-inch skillet, heat oil (over medium-high heat) and I Can't Believe It's Not Butter!® Spread and cook chicken 10 minutes or until golden, turning once. Transfer chicken to 13×9-inch baking dish and bake uncovered 15 minutes or until chicken is thoroughly cooked in center. Remove toothpicks before serving.   *Makes about 6 servings*

Easy Chicken Pot Pie

2 cups cut-up cooked chicken
1 package (10 ounces) frozen mixed vegetables, thawed
1¼ cups milk
  1 envelope LIPTON® RECIPE SECRETS® Golden Onion Soup Mix*
  1 pie crust or pastry for single-crust pie

*Also terrific with LIPTON® RECIPE SECRETS® Savory Herb with Garlic Soup Mix.

1. Preheat oven to 400°F. In 9-inch pie plate, combine chicken and vegetables; set aside.

2. In small saucepan, bring milk and soup mix to a boil over medium heat, stirring occasionally. Cook 1 minute. Stir into chicken mixture.

3. Top with pie crust. Press pastry around edge of pie plate to seal; trim excess pastry, then flute edges. With tip of knife, make small slits in pastry.

4. Bake uncovered 35 minutes or until crust is golden.

Makes about 4 servings

Menu Suggestion: *Serve with your favorite LIPTON® Soup and LIPTON® Iced Tea.*

APPETIZING
CHICKEN

18

Herbed Chicken & Vegetables

2 medium all-purpose potatoes, thinly sliced (about 1 pound)
2 medium carrots, sliced
4 bone-in chicken pieces (about 2 pounds)
1 envelope LIPTON® RECIPE SECRETS® Savory Herb with Garlic Soup Mix
⅓ cup water
1 tablespoon BERTOLLI® Olive Oil

1. Preheat oven to 425°F. In broiler pan without the rack, place potatoes and carrots; arrange chicken on top. Pour soup mix blended with water and oil over chicken and vegetables.

2. Bake uncovered 40 minutes or until chicken is thoroughly cooked, juices run clear and vegetables are tender.   *Makes 4 servings*

Slow Cooker Method: *In slow cooker, layer potatoes, carrots then chicken. Pour soup mix blended with water and oil over chicken and vegetables. Cook covered on HIGH 4 hours or LOW 6 to 8 hours.*

APPETIZING CHICKEN

Garlic Chicken Melt

4 boneless, skinless chicken breast halves (about 1¼ pounds)
1 envelope LIPTON® RECIPE SECRETS® Savory Herb with Garlic Soup Mix
1 can (14 ounces) diced tomatoes, undrained or 1 large tomato, chopped
1 tablespoon BERTOLLI® Olive Oil
½ cup shredded mozzarella or Monterey Jack cheese (about 2 ounces)

1. Preheat oven to 375°F. In 13×9-inch baking or roasting pan, arrange chicken. Pour soup mix blended with tomatoes and oil over chicken.

2. Bake uncovered 25 minutes or until chicken is thoroughly cooked.

3. Sprinkle with mozzarella cheese and bake an additional 2 minutes or until cheese is melted. *Makes 4 servings*

APPETIZING CHICKEN

20

Roasted Chicken & Garlic Provençale

1 envelope LIPTON® RECIPE SECRETS® Savory Herb with Garlic Soup Mix
3 tablespoons BERTOLLI® Olive Oil
2 tablespoons water
1 tablespoon white wine vinegar (optional)
1 (2½- to 3-pound) chicken, cut into serving pieces
1 large onion, cut into 8 wedges
1 large tomato, cut into 8 wedges

1. Preheat oven to 425°F. In small bowl, blend soup mix, oil, water and vinegar.

2. In bottom of broiler pan without rack, arrange chicken, onion and tomato. Evenly pour soup mixture over chicken and vegetables.

3. Roast 45 minutes or until chicken is thoroughly cooked.

Makes 4 servings

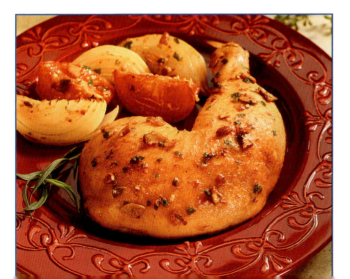

Crispy Garlic Chicken

1 envelope LIPTON® RECIPE SECRETS® Savory Herb with Garlic Soup Mix*

⅓ cup HELLMANN'S® or BEST FOODS® Real Mayonnaise

¼ cup grated Parmesan cheese

6 boneless, skinless chicken breast halves (about 1¾ pounds)

2 tablespoons plain dry bread crumbs

Also terrific with LIPTON® RECIPE SECRETS® Onion Soup Mix

1. Preheat oven to 400°F. In medium bowl, combine soup mix, mayonnaise and cheese; set aside.

2. On baking sheet, arrange chicken. Evenly top chicken with soup mixture, then evenly sprinkle with bread crumbs.

3. Bake uncovered 20 minutes or until chicken is thoroughly cooked.

Makes 4 servings

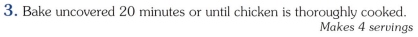

Chicken & Broccoli with Garlic Sauce

2 tablespoons BERTOLLI® Olive Oil
4 boneless, skinless chicken breast halves (about 1¼ pounds)
1 package (10 ounces) frozen broccoli florets, thawed
1 envelope LIPTON® RECIPE SECRETS® Savory Herb with Garlic Soup Mix
1 cup water
3 tablespoons orange juice
1 teaspoon soy sauce

1. In 12-inch nonstick skillet, heat oil over medium-high heat and brown chicken. Remove chicken and set aside.

2. In same skillet, add broccoli and soup mix blended with water, orange juice and soy sauce. Bring to a boil over high heat.

3. Return chicken to skillet. Reduce heat to low and simmer covered 10 minutes or until chicken is thoroughly cooked. Serve, if desired, over hot cooked rice. *Makes 4 servings*

Garlic Pork Chops

6 bone-in pork chops, ¾ inch thick
1 envelope LIPTON® RECIPE SECRETS® Savory Herb with Garlic Soup Mix
2 tablespoons vegetable oil
½ cup hot water

1. Preheat oven to 425°F. In broiler pan, without the rack, arrange chops. Brush both sides of chops with soup mix combined with oil.

2. Bake chops 25 minutes or until done.

3. Remove chops to serving platter. Add hot water to pan and stir, scraping brown bits from bottom of pan. Serve sauce over chops.

Makes 4 servings

PLEASING PORK

Onion-Baked Pork Chops

1 envelope LIPTON® RECIPE SECRETS® Golden Onion Soup Mix*
⅓ cup plain dry bread crumbs
4 pork chops, 1 inch thick (about 3 pounds)
1 egg, well beaten

Also terrific with LIPTON® RECIPE SECRETS® Onion or Savory Herb with Garlic Soup Mix.

1. Preheat oven to 400°F. In small bowl, combine soup mix and bread crumbs. Dip chops in egg, then bread crumb mixture until evenly coated.

2. Arrange chops on baking sheet.

3. Bake uncovered 20 minutes or until done, turning once.

Makes 4 servings

PLEASING PORK

Onion-Apple Glazed Pork Tenderloin

1 (1½- to 2-pound) boneless pork tenderloin
Ground black pepper
2 tablespoons BERTOLLI® Olive Oil, divided
1 envelope LIPTON® RECIPE SECRETS® Onion Soup Mix
½ cup apple juice
2 tablespoons firmly packed brown sugar
¾ cup water
¼ cup dry red wine or water
1 tablespoon all-purpose flour

1. Preheat oven to 425°F. In small roasting pan or baking pan, arrange pork. Season with pepper and rub with 1 tablespoon olive oil. Roast uncovered 10 minutes.

2. Meanwhile, in small bowl, combine remaining 1 tablespoon olive oil, soup mix, apple juice and brown sugar. Pour over pork and continue roasting 10 minutes or until desired doneness. Remove pork to serving platter; cover with aluminum foil.

3. Place roasting pan over medium-high heat and bring pan juices to a boil, scraping up any browned bits from bottom of pan. Stir in water, wine and flour; boil, stirring constantly, 1 minute or until thickened. To serve, thinly slice pork and serve with gravy.

Makes 4 to 6 servings

PLEASING PORK

Asian Shrimp & Steak Kabobs

1 envelope LIPTON® RECIPE SECRETS® Savory Herb with Garlic or Onion Soup Mix
¼ cup soy sauce
¼ cup lemon juice
¼ cup BERTOLLI® Olive Oil
¼ cup honey
½ pound uncooked medium shrimp, peeled and deveined
½ pound boneless sirloin steak, cut into 1-inch cubes
16 cherry tomatoes
2 cups mushroom caps
1 medium green bell pepper, cut into chunks

1. In 13×9-inch glass baking dish, blend soup mix, soy sauce, lemon juice, oil and honey; set aside.

2. On skewers, alternately thread shrimp, steak, tomatoes, mushrooms and green pepper. Add prepared skewers to baking dish; turn to coat. Cover and marinate in refrigerator, turning skewers occasionally, at least 2 hours. Remove prepared skewers, reserving marinade.

3. Grill or broil, turning and basting frequently with reserved marinade, until shrimp turn pink and steak is cooked to desired doneness. Do not baste with marinade during last 5 minutes of cooking.   *Makes about 8 servings*

DELICIOUS BEEF

Harvest Pot Roast with Sweet Potatoes

1 envelope LIPTON® RECIPE SECRETS® Onion Soup Mix
1½ cups water
¼ cup soy sauce
2 tablespoons firmly packed dark brown sugar
1 teaspoon ground ginger (optional)
1 (3- to 3½-pound) boneless pot roast (rump, chuck or round)
4 large sweet potatoes, peeled, if desired, and cut into large chunks
3 tablespoons water
2 tablespoons all-purpose flour

1. Preheat oven to 325°F. In Dutch oven or 5-quart heavy ovenproof saucepot, combine soup mix, water, soy sauce, brown sugar and ginger; add roast.

2. Cover and bake 1 hour 45 minutes.

3. Add potatoes and bake covered an additional 45 minutes or until beef and potatoes are tender. Remove roast and potatoes to serving platter and keep warm; reserve juices.

4. In small cup, with wire whisk, blend water and flour. In same Dutch oven, add flour mixture to reserved juices. Bring to a boil over high heat. Boil, stirring occasionally, 2 minutes. Serve with roast and potatoes. *Makes 6 servings*

DELICIOUS BEEF

Golden Glazed Flank Steak

1 envelope LIPTON® RECIPE SECRETS® Onion Soup Mix*
1 jar (12 ounces) apricot or peach preserves
½ cup water
1 beef flank steak (about 2 pounds), cut into thin strips
2 medium green, red and/or yellow bell peppers, sliced
   Hot cooked rice

Also terrific with LIPTON® RECIPE SECRETS® Onion Mushroom Soup Mix.

1. In small bowl, combine soup mix, preserves and water; set aside.

2. On heavy-duty aluminum foil or in bottom of broiler pan with rack removed, arrange steak and green peppers; top with soup mixture.

3. Broil, turning steak and vegetables once, until steak is done. Serve over hot rice.   *Makes 8 servings*

DELICIOUS BEEF

Hearty BBQ Beef Sandwiches

1 envelope LIPTON® RECIPE SECRETS® Onion Soup Mix
2 cups water
½ cup chili sauce
¼ cup firmly packed light brown sugar
1 (3-pound) boneless chuck roast
8 kaiser rolls or hamburger buns, toasted

1. Preheat oven to 325°F. In Dutch oven or 5-quart heavy ovenproof saucepot, combine soup mix, water, chili sauce and sugar; add roast.

2. Cover and bake 3 hours or until roast is tender.

3. Remove roast; reserve juices. Bring reserved juices to a boil over high heat. Boil 4 minutes.

4. Meanwhile, with fork, shred roast. Stir roast into reserved juices and simmer, stirring frequently, 1 minute. Serve on rolls.

Makes 8 servings

Recipe Tip: *Always measure brown sugar in a dry measure cup and pack down firmly. To soften hardened brown sugar, place in glass bowl with 1 slice of bread. Cover with plastic wrap and microwave at HIGH 30 to 40 seconds. Let stand 30 seconds; stir. Remove bread.*

DELICIOUS BEEF

Southwestern Beef Stew

1 tablespoon plus 1 teaspoon BERTOLLI® Olive Oil, divided
1½ pounds boneless beef chuck, cut into 1-inch cubes
1 can (4 ounces) chopped green chilies, drained
2 large cloves garlic, finely chopped
1 teaspoon ground cumin (optional)
1 can (14 to 16 ounces) whole or plum tomatoes, undrained and
    chopped
1 envelope LIPTON® RECIPE SECRETS® Onion Soup Mix
1 cup water
1 package (10 ounces) frozen cut okra or green beans, thawed
1 large red or green bell pepper, cut into 1-inch pieces
4 frozen half-ears corn-on-the-cob, thawed and each cut into
    3 round pieces
    Fresh cilantro (optional)

In 5-quart Dutch oven or heavy saucepot, heat 1 tablespoon oil over medium-high heat and brown ½ of the beef; remove and set aside. Repeat with remaining beef. In same Dutch oven, heat remaining 1 teaspoon oil over medium heat and cook chilies, garlic and cumin, stirring constantly, 3 minutes. Return beef to Dutch oven. Stir in tomatoes and soup mix blended with water. Bring to a boil over high heat. Reduce heat to low and simmer covered, stirring occasionally, 1 hour. Stir in okra, red pepper and corn. Bring to a boil over high heat. Reduce heat to low and simmer covered, stirring occasionally, 30 minutes or until meat is tender. Garnish with cilantro.

Makes about 6 servings

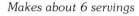

DELICIOUS BEEF

31

Skillet Beef & Broccoli

1 tablespoon BERTOLLI® Olive Oil
1 pound sirloin steak, cut into 1-inch strips
1 package (10 ounces) frozen broccoli florets, thawed
1 envelope LIPTON® RECIPE SECRETS® Onion Soup Mix*
1¼ cups water
1 tablespoon firmly packed brown sugar
1 tablespoon soy sauce

Also terrific with LIPTON® RECIPE SECRETS® Onion Mushroom Soup Mix.

1. In 12-inch nonstick skillet, heat oil over medium-high heat and brown steak, stirring occasionally, in two batches. Remove steak from skillet and set aside.

2. Stir in broccoli and soup mix blended with water, brown sugar and soy sauce. Bring to a boil over high heat. Reduce heat to low and simmer uncovered, stirring occasionally, 2 minutes.

3. Return steak to skillet and cook 1 minute or until steak is done. Serve, if desired, with hot cooked rice.   *Makes 4 servings*

DELICIOUS BEEF

Lipton® Onion Burgers

1 envelope LIPTON® RECIPE SECRETS® Onion Soup Mix*
2 pounds ground beef
½ cup water

Also terrific with LIPTON® RECIPE SECRETS® Beefy Onion, Onion Mushroom, Beefy Mushroom, Savory Herb with Garlic or Ranch Soup Mix.

1. In large bowl, combine all ingredients; shape into 8 patties.

2. Grill or broil until done.   *Makes about 8 servings*

DELICIOUS BEEF

33

Onion Sloppy Joes

1½ pounds ground beef
  1 envelope LIPTON® RECIPE SECRETS® Onion Soup Mix
  1 cup water
  1 cup ketchup
  2 tablespoons firmly packed brown sugar

1. In 10-inch skillet, brown ground beef over medium-high heat; drain.

2. Stir in remaining ingredients. Bring to a boil over high heat.

3. Reduce heat to low and simmer uncovered, stirring occasionally, 8 minutes or until mixture thickens. Serve, if desired, on hoagie rolls or hamburger buns.   *Makes about 6 servings*

Menu Suggestion: *Serve with a lettuce and tomato salad, tortilla chips and ice cream with a choice of toppings.*

Oven-Baked Stew

   2 pounds boneless beef chuck or round steak, cut into 1-inch cubes
 ¼ cup all-purpose flour
1⅓ cups sliced carrots
   1 can (14 to 16 ounces) whole peeled tomatoes, undrained and
        chopped
   1 envelope LIPTON® RECIPE SECRETS® Onion Soup Mix*
 ½ cup dry red wine or water
   1 cup fresh or canned sliced mushrooms
   1 package (8 ounces) medium or broad egg noodles, cooked and
        drained

*Also terrific with LIPTON® RECIPE SECRETS® Beefy Onion, Onion Mushroom or
Beefy Mushroom Soup Mix.*

1. Preheat oven to 425°F. In 2½-quart shallow casserole, toss beef
with flour, then bake uncovered 20 minutes, stirring once.

2. *Reduce heat to 350°F.* Stir in carrots, tomatoes, soup mix and
wine.

3. Bake covered 1½ hours or until beef is tender. Stir in mushrooms
and bake covered an additional 10 minutes. Serve over hot noodles.
                                                    Makes 8 servings

DELICIOUS BEEF

Garlic Shrimp with Wilted Spinach

2 teaspoons BERTOLLI® Olive Oil
1 pound uncooked medium shrimp, peeled and deveined
¼ cup diagonally sliced green onions
2 tablespoons sherry or dry white wine (optional)
1 envelope LIPTON® RECIPE SECRETS® Savory Herb with Garlic Soup Mix*
1½ cups water
1 large tomato, diced
2 cups fresh trimmed spinach leaves (about 4 ounces)
¼ cup chopped unsalted cashews (optional)

Also terrific with Lipton® Recipe Secrets® Golden Onion Soup Mix.

1. In 12-inch skillet, heat oil over medium heat and cook shrimp 2 minutes or until pink. Remove and set aside.

2. In same skillet, cook green onions, stirring occasionally, 2 minutes or until slightly soft. Add sherry and bring to a boil over high heat, stirring frequently. Stir in soup mix blended with water. Bring to a boil over high heat. Reduce heat to low and simmer 5 minutes or until sauce is thickened. Stir in tomato and spinach. Simmer covered, stirring once, 3 minutes or until spinach is cooked. Return shrimp to skillet and cook 1 minute or until heated through. Sprinkle with cashews. *Makes about 4 servings*

Seafood Salad Sandwiches

1 envelope LIPTON® RECIPE SECRETS® Vegetable Soup Mix
¾ cup sour cream
½ cup chopped celery
¼ cup HELLMANN'S® or BEST FOODS® Real Mayonnaise
1 tablespoon fresh or frozen chopped chives (optional)
1 teaspoon lemon juice
   Hot pepper sauce to taste
⅛ teaspoon ground black pepper
2 packages (6 ounces each) frozen crabmeat, thawed and well
   drained*
4 hard rolls, halved
   Lettuce leaves

Variations: Use 1 package (12 ounces) frozen cleaned shrimp, cooked and coarsely chopped; or 2 packages (8 ounces each) sea legs, thawed, drained and chopped; or 1 can (12 ounces) tuna, drained and flaked; or 2 cans (about 4 ounces each) medium or large shrimp, drained and chopped; or 2 cans (6 ounces each) crabmeat, drained and flaked.

In large bowl, blend soup mix, sour cream, celery, mayonnaise, chives, lemon juice, hot pepper sauce and pepper. Stir in crabmeat; chill. To serve, line rolls with lettuce, then fill with crab mixture.

Makes 4 sandwiches

Summer Vegetable & Fish Bundles

4 fish fillets (about 1 pound)
1 pound thinly sliced vegetables*
1 envelope LIPTON® RECIPE SECRETS® Savory Herb with Garlic or
   Golden Onion Soup Mix
½ cup water

*Use any combination of the following: thinly sliced mushrooms, zucchini,
yellow squash or tomatoes.*

On two 18×18-inch pieces heavy-duty aluminum foil, divide fish equally; top with vegetables. Evenly pour soup mix blended with water over fish. Wrap foil loosely around fillets and vegetables, sealing edges airtight with double fold. Grill or broil seam side up 15 minutes or until fish flakes.   *Makes about 4 servings*

Menu Suggestion: *Serve over hot cooked rice with Lipton® Iced Tea mixed with a splash of cranberry juice cocktail.*

**LUSCIOUS
SEAFOOD**

Easy Fried Rice

¼ cup BERTOLLI® Olive Oil
4 cups cooked rice
2 cloves garlic, finely chopped
1 envelope LIPTON® RECIPE SECRETS® Onion Mushroom Soup Mix
½ cup water
1 tablespoon soy sauce
1 cup frozen peas and carrots, partially thawed
2 eggs, lightly beaten

1. In 12-inch nonstick skillet, heat oil over medium-high heat and cook rice, stirring constantly, 2 minutes or until rice is heated through. Stir in garlic.

2. Stir in soup mix blended with water and soy sauce and cook 1 minute. Stir in peas and carrots and cook 2 minutes or until heated through.

3. Make a well in center of rice and quickly stir in eggs until cooked.

Makes 4 servings

**SATISFYING
SIDES**

Garlic Mashed Potatoes

6 medium all-purpose potatoes, peeled, if desired, and cut into chunks (about 3 pounds)

Water

1 envelope LIPTON® RECIPE SECRETS® Savory Herb with Garlic Soup Mix*

½ cup milk

½ cup I CAN'T BELIEVE IT'S NOT BUTTER!® Spread

Also terrific with LIPTON® RECIPE SECRETS® Onion or Golden Onion Soup Mix.

1. In 4-quart saucepan, cover potatoes with water; bring to a boil.

2. Reduce heat to low and simmer uncovered 20 minutes or until potatoes are very tender; drain.

3. Return potatoes to saucepan, then mash. Stir in remaining ingredients.
Makes 8 servings

Simply Delicious Pasta Primavera

¼ cup margarine or butter
1 envelope LIPTON® RECIPE SECRETS® Vegetable Soup Mix
1½ cups milk
8 ounces linguine or spaghetti, cooked and drained
¼ cup grated Parmesan cheese (about 1 ounce)

1. In medium saucepan, melt margarine over medium heat and stir in soup mix and milk. Bring just to a boil over high heat.

2. Reduce heat to low and simmer uncovered, stirring occasionally, 10 minutes or until vegetables are tender. Toss hot linguine with sauce and Parmesan cheese. *Makes 4 servings*

Vegetable Potato Salad

1 envelope LIPTON® RECIPE SECRETS® Vegetable Soup Mix
1 cup HELLMANN'S® or BEST FOODS® Mayonnaise
2 teaspoons white vinegar
2 pounds red or all-purpose potatoes, cooked and cut into chunks
¼ cup finely chopped red onion (optional)

1. In large bowl, combine soup mix, mayonnaise and vinegar.

2. Add potatoes and onion; toss well. Chill 2 hours.

Makes 6 servings

Savory Skillet Broccoli

1 tablespoon BERTOLLI® Olive Oil
6 cups fresh broccoli florets *or* 1 pound green beans, trimmed
1 envelope LIPTON® RECIPE SECRETS® Golden Onion Soup Mix*
1½ cups water

*Also terrific with LIPTON® RECIPE SECRETS® Onion Mushroom Soup Mix.

1. In 12-inch skillet, heat oil over medium-high heat and cook broccoli, stirring occasionally, 2 minutes.

2. Stir in soup mix blended with water. Bring to a boil over high heat.

3. Reduce heat to medium-low and simmer covered 6 minutes or until broccoli is tender. *Makes 4 servings*

**SATISFYING
SIDES**

Roasted Idaho & Sweet Potatoes

1 envelope LIPTON® RECIPE SECRETS® Onion Soup Mix
2 medium all-purpose potatoes, peeled, if desired, and cut into large chunks (about 1 pound)
2 medium sweet potatoes or yams, peeled, if desired, and cut into large chunks (about 1 pound)
¼ cup BERTOLLI® Olive Oil

1. Preheat oven to 425°F. In large plastic bag or bowl, combine all ingredients. Close bag and shake, or toss in bowl, until potatoes are evenly coated.

2. In 13×9-inch baking or roasting pan, arrange potatoes; discard bag.

3. Bake uncovered, stirring occasionally, 40 minutes or until potatoes are tender and golden.   *Makes 4 servings*

Couscous with Vegetables in Savory Broth

2 tablespoons I CAN'T BELIEVE IT'S NOT BUTTER!® Spread
1 large onion, sliced
½ cup dry white wine or water
1 cup sliced carrots
1 medium zucchini, sliced
1 small red or green bell pepper, sliced
1 envelope LIPTON® RECIPE SECRETS® Savory Herb with Garlic Soup Mix
2 cups water
1⅓ cups (8 ounces) couscous, cooked*

Variation: Use hot cooked penne or ziti pasta.

In 12-inch skillet, melt I Can't Believe It's Not Butter!® Spread over medium heat and cook onion, stirring occasionally, 5 minutes or until golden. Add wine and boil over high heat 1 minute. Stir in carrots, zucchini, red pepper and soup mix blended with water. Bring to a boil over high heat. Reduce heat to low and simmer uncovered, stirring occasionally, 15 minutes. To serve, spoon over hot couscous.

Makes about 5 servings

Menu Suggestion: *Serve with a mixed green salad and sliced fresh fruit drizzled with honey for dessert.*

Savory Onion Cheese Tart

1 envelope LIPTON® RECIPE SECRETS® Golden Onion Soup Mix
1 cup milk
1 egg, lightly beaten
½ teaspoon rosemary leaves
1 package (8 ounces) mozzarella cheese, shredded
1 package (15 ounces) refrigerated pie crusts for 2 (9-inch) crusts

In small bowl, thoroughly blend soup mix, milk, egg and rosemary. Stir in cheese. Freeze 1 hour or refrigerate at least 2 hours until mixture is slightly thickened and not runny.

Preheat oven to 375°F. On two aluminum-foil-lined baking sheets, unfold crusts. Fold crust edges over 1 inch to form rim. Brush, if desired, with 1 egg yolk beaten with 2 tablespoons water. Fill center of each prepared crust with half soup mixture; spread evenly to rim. Bake 25 minutes or until crusts are golden brown. To serve, cut into wedges

Makes 2 tarts

Freezing/Reheating Directions: *Tarts can be baked, then frozen. Simply wrap in heavy-duty aluminum foil; freeze. To reheat, unwrap and bake at 350°F until heated through.*

Pie Crusts